STROUD
AND THE FIVE VALLEYS
IN OLD PHOTOGRAPHS
A SECOND SELECTION

STROUD
AND THE FIVE VALLEYS
IN OLD PHOTOGRAPHS
A SECOND SELECTION

COLLECTED BY

S.J. GARDINER AND L.C. PADIN

Stanley J Gardiner

Lionel C. Padin

ALAN SUTTON
1987

Alan Sutton Publishing Limited
Brunswick Road · Gloucester

First published 1987

British Library Cataloguing in Publication Data

Stroud and the Five Valleys in old
photographs : a second selection.
1. Stroud (Gloucestershire : District) —
Social; life and customs — Pictorial
works
I. Padin, L.C.   II. Gardiner, S.J.
942.4′19081′0222   DA670.S8

ISBN 0-86299-465-0

Typesetting and origination by
Alan Sutton Publishing Limited.
Printed in Great Britain by
WBC Print Limited · Bristol.

CONTENTS

INTRODUCTION

In our first book it proved impossible to include all aspects of past scenes in and around Stroud due to lack of space and also, in no small way, to the enthusiasm of the 'camera clickers' of yesteryear, who delighted in recording so many facets of life as it was being played around them.

Once again we hope that the selection of old photographs shown here will stimulate readers to seek out the spots from which they were taken and compare them with the current scene. Perhaps the nostalgic verdict will be that the change has been for the worse.

We must apologise to the avid transport 'buffs' for not including any transport pictures in this selection. We feel we must have more than enough photographs of all aspects of transport from the local area to justify a separate volume which we hope our publishers will issue in the future.

Once again we are indebted to the many people who have loaned, and who still loan postcards, albums etc. to us to copy, often together with a wealth of information relating to them. We pay tribute to those professional photographers of the Stroud area – Colville, Comley, Elliott, Lee, Loveland, Major, Merrett, Moss, Peckham, Restall, Richards, Smith, Stone and the national professionals – Frith and Taunt. Neither must we forget to acknowledge our debt to those traders who commissioned the professionals to print their efforts as postcards for sale to the general public, such as Olpin of Ebley, Collins & Lee of Stroud, Wiley & Timbrell of Stonehouse, Jones of Minchinhampton, Smart & Cook of Chalford and Conway of Nailsworth to name but a few.

Our grateful thanks also to Jack Anderson, Neville Crawford, John Denley, Wilf Gardner, Fred Hammond and Oliver Jeffery who have given so freely of their extensive knowledge and memories of various parts of the district; and to the late Geoffrey Sanders who was forever helpful.

Finally, our grateful thanks to our typist, Mrs Joan Sammons, for once again interpreting our manuscript.

Stroud – Central

The street scene in Stroud has changed quite considerably during the last 40 years, if only in the replacement of old shop fronts with modern ones; family businesses with chainstores and a surfeit of Building Societies, Estate and Travel Agents, all depicting a more affluent and more mobile way of life. In those 40 years the town became stifled by an excess of internal combustion-engined, wheeled monsters of all sizes. Happily, the pendulum is now swinging the other way so that once more the pedestrian might be thought worthy of chief place in the street scene, as he obviously was in many of the pictures which follow.

BEECHES GREEN, showing the path which connects the Cheltenham Road, near the Old Police Station, with Folly Lane. The photograph was taken by Elliott c. 1895, shortly before the comparatively new Urban District Council erected a new fence.

BEECHES GREEN – a view from where the roundabout is today c. 1910–12. The original was one of a series called *The Streets of Stroud* issued by W.H. Collins of High Street (see p. 17). On the right, the Petty Sessional Court extension to the Police Station was opened in October 1908. On the left, the entrance to Badbrook House, which was demolished in the 1960s to make way for the Merrywalks reconstruction.

AN EDWARDIAN VIEW FROM STATION VIADUCT TOWARDS BEECHES GREEN showing the long gardens of many of the Rowcroft Buildings. In the centre – Badbrook Mills – the site of which is now covered by the multi-storey car park, bus station, etc. To the right of the Mill chimney, partly obscured by a tree, is Badbrook House.

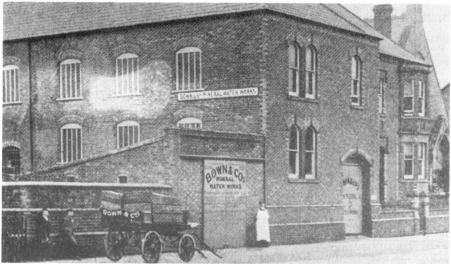

THE MINERAL WATER WORKS OF BOWN & CO. in Lansdown in 1898. They had a retail shop at the south end of Lansdown where Sew & So have their shop today. The company moved to their present site in Slad Road after the Second World War. This building is now used by Bailey's haulage firm. The partly-obscured building on the extreme right was opened in 1876 as a Unitarian Chapel. In 1894 it became Stroud's second Baptist Church under the Revd W. Soper, who had resigned from the Pastorate of John Street Baptist Church on doctrinal grounds. In 1907 the two Churches re-united. This building then became Spot's Cinema for many years and later still the Liberal Club. It is now a ballroom and dance school.

ONE OF THE BEST-KNOWN CROSSROADS IN THE TOWN at the top of Gloucester Street. For years, from at least the 1920s until the advent of the one-way system, the 'Bobby' on point duty was a familiar sight. Many will recall that martinet of point duty – 'Banger' Yates. The cars in this photograph suggest a mid 1930s date.

KING STREET FROM LANSDOWN. An Edwardian scene issued by Tomkins & Barrett, who were Swindon confectioners, as a coloured postcard. The card was posted on 28 April 1913. T & B cards always carried a short description of the location. In this photograph, on the left, is the hat shop of Gardner, next the Dale Forty (Cheltenham) Music Shop, next to that would have been Shelton's – Fine Art dealers, and beyond, by the covered wagon, S.M. Strange – Grocer & Fruiterer. On the right, the sign of the Green Dragon Inn and beyond that, on the corner of Bath Street where Hodges is today, would have been Chew – Ironmonger.

A 1920s VIEW OF KING STREET FROM THE PARADE. The junction with George Street often required a point duty policeman as well. Just beyond the EXIT to the Picture House, where the window cleaner has his ladder, is Woolworths. The projecting sign beyond was for Tuck's Cafe. Tapper House Furnisher had a warehouse in Bath Road (see p. 37).

A SKETCH OF THE LOWER HIGH STREET issued as a postcard in Victorian times. The dress suggests that this depicts a scene of the 1840s. Nos 9 & 10 would be in the area of the newsagents shop today, making the wider part of the street approximately opposite the Bedford Arms Inn.

AN EDWARDIAN VIEW OF THE LOWER HIGH STREET, from the region of Bedford Street. Compare the windows with the previous picture. The shops on the right, Maypole Groceries, a Stead & Simpson shoe shop and No. 62, a tobacconist, are now part of the recently renovated section of the street.

KENDRICK STREET, the junction with the High Street decorated for the 1907 Agricultural Show – the arch straddling the street where E & S shops are today. These arches were a common and elaborate feature of the shows. Hilliers, Bacon Curers of Newmarket, Nailsworth, moved their shop to Russell Street after the Second World War to approximately where the Fruiterers are today. The Victorian postbox on the right pavement is still there.

THE OLD ALMSHOUSES IN CHURCH STREET in 1903, bequeathed by Thomas Webb of The Hill in 1642 for the housing and upbringing etc. of four poor children until they could be apprenticed. This bequest was later joined with that of Wyndowe. The recipients' clothing was made of red cloth and they were generally called 'Red Boys.' They were educated at the school in the Market House. This aspect of the charity had lapsed by the time of this picture.

THE SAME AREA C. 1960. The Almshouses have been demolished but a building at the back remains, which would then have been Gallie's Garage. Before that, it housed the Mineral Water Department of the Cotswold Stores and in the middle of the last century it was a small brewery. It was here, apparently, c. 1779, that the Bath Theatrical Company set up a small theatre, where the celebrated eighteenth-century actress Mrs Siddons once played. Rodney House on the left was also built by Thomas Webb in 1634 and was the home of Dr Paine in the latter half of the last century.

UPPER SWAN LANE c. 1960. The area on the right is now part of the medieval building's forecourt. Some readers may recall that tin-smithing and umbrella repairing were carried on in the first two small shops.

UPPER HIGH STREET in the late 1920s. W.H. Collins stands where Marriotts is now. Opposite was where James Lee, another Stroud publisher of postcards, had his shop. Halfords then had their shop at the corner of Church Street where Elliotts Steam Printing Works had been. It is now part of Whitchers Menswear.

ACRE STREET at its junction with Chapel Street, probably c 1900. All these buildings have now been replaced by the modern estate.

THE CROSS c. 1900. The Dolphin Fountain, topped by the lamp, stood where the mini-roundabout is today. The buildings of Guest, draper and milliner, and Wood, china etc. were demolished and replaced in 1931 by the Headquarters of the Stroud Co-op, which now houses a variety of businesses. Nelson Street is to the right and Silver Street, as it was then, is to the left.

MIDDLE STREET probably c 1912. The wall on the right has been partly demolished for Sutton's shop and nursery business.

IN LONDON ROAD c. 1895, from the entrance to today's car park. The building on the left behind the child is now the London Hotel. The road is no wider today!

THE ORIGINAL LONDON ROAD CAR PARK c. 1933 where even buses could park. A busy GWR goods yard in the background, now the lower car park. A facetious question – could the hut be the one that is still there today?

Yes, there was an air-raid shelter on the Subscription Rooms forecourt in the Second World War! Here a few people are queuing for the Chalford bus.

Stroud, George Street.

A VIEW ALONG GEORGE STREET C. 1905. At the end of the street on the right is the Royal George Hotel and to its left the low roof of the George Tap Inn where the entrance to the precinct is now.

UPPER RUSSELL STREET in 1905. The entrance on the left, by the Wooden Studio, was later the entrance to Steels Garage's workshops, which is approximately where the car ramp to the Stroud and Swindon Building Society's offices is today. Next along is Wells the Jewellers, then Pearce's the Saddlers and the next shop eventually became the Red & White Bus Company office. Beyond that is Comley's the Photographers.

LOWER RUSSELL STREET probably c. 1912–15. Beyond the solitary horse and cart, which is standing by the Railway Hotel, is the end of Rowcroft House where part of Lloyds Bank now stands.

KENDRICK STREET C. 1901–2. On the corner with Threadneedle Street is Walters Cake Shop replacing that of R.T. Smith – GWR Carriers. Opposite where the pet shop is today, was Cratchley's China and Glass Emporium. The shop seen in High Street, facing Kendrick Street, was a wine & spirit merchants.

KING STREET PARADE with another Agricultural Show arch over King Street, possibly for the 1907 show again. The building of this seems to have been undertaken by Philip Ford & Son. Just disappearing up George Street is a wagon of Thos. Dangerfield, a Stroud/Gloucester carrier. The business is still in existence.

KING STREET PARADE AND ROWCROFT in the period 1895–1901 with plenty of horse traffic in evidence. The recently erected (1895) statue to George Holloway is on the left. The large sacks on the one wagon could be woolsacks. Prominent on the railway bridge is the advert for Godsell & Son of Salmon Springs Brewery. The structure on the right was to disappear in the 1930s reconstruction of Lloyds Bank.

THE JUNCTION OF ROWCROFT AND THE CAINSCROSS ROAD in 1960 with the Stroud Brewery office frontage on the right. The buildings on the left housed the Bottling and Mineral Waters Plant. The office block was built by George Drew of Chalford in 1901. In the background, where the road curves out of sight by the present day filling station, is the roof of Far Hill House (see p. 33).

SECTION TWO

Stroud – The Old Urban District

For almost 40 years, until local government re-organisation in 1974, the old Urban District of Stroud stretched roughly from Bowbridge to Ebley and from Lightpill for a mile along the Cheltenham Road (A46). With the inclusion of the Cainscross and much of the Rodborough civil parishes within the urban boundary in 1936, the housing expansion of Stroud to the north-west and to the south, with encroachment into the Rural District, perhaps became inevitable. This has caused great changes to the scene, in for example, the Cashes Green and Lightpill areas, as will be obvious to those who travelled on the old railcar, or the 'Dudbridge Donkey'. But the same could have been said 60 years ago about the changed scene in the Horns Road, Uplands and Rodborough areas.

THE JUNCTION OF FOXMOOR LANE WITH THE A419 AT EBLEY with crowds awaiting the 1919 Peace Day Parade. The name of the Fire Brigade that occupied the centre of the road is not known.

GERMAN GUN IN VICTORY PARK, CAINSCROSS.

THIS RELIC FROM WORLD WAR I was a feature of Victory Park, Cainscross, between the wars.

HAYMAKING AT EBLEY, at the rear of the old abbatoir site, in Edwardian days.

CASHES GREEN IN RURAL DAYS, possibly 1920s – fields that are now built over. The small underpass bridge, lower left, is believed to be the one which has been converted into a 'culverted underpass'.

THE CROSSROADS AT CAINSCROSS c. 1912–20, with the White Horse Inn on the left. The dual carriageway to the roundabout now replaces the buildings on the right.

THE JUNCTION OF PAGANHILL LANE AND STRATFORD ROAD, probably 1920s.

THE STRATFORD PARK SWIMMING POOL in use just before the Second World War. The park was purchased by Stroud UDC early in 1936 and approval for the building of the pool given by the MOH in May, 1936.

A TRANQUIL VIEW from Beeches Green towards the Stratford Road junction c. 1900. No fear of traffic for big sister taking baby in the pushchair – or is it a lucky girl with a large doll?

UPLANDS FROM THE BELLVUE ROAD AREA 1908–9. Upper right, scaffolding surrounds the new church, the foundation stone of which was laid on 30 June 1908 by Viscount St Aldwyn. Lower left is the roofless mill which housed Idloes Cabinet Works, gutted by fire in December 1905.

CAINSCROSS ROAD c. 1900. On the left is the corner of Far Hill House which stood where the long-stay car-park is today.

FAR HILL HOUSE in the 1920s when it would have been used by the Cotswold Stores Group as their main distribution centre for the numerous general stores they owned in the district. The house was built by Benjamin Grazebrook in the eighteenth century; his son Joseph lived there until his death in 1843, at the age of 92. Benjamin was responsible for supplying piped water from Gainey's Well to Upper Stroud in 1770 and was also a partner in one of Stroud's earliest banks – the Stroud Bank. The house was purchased by the District Council and considered for conversion and enlargement to serve as headquarters for the present Stroud District Council. After they rejected this idea, it was demolished.

UPPER DORINGTON TERRACE, Stroud, in the early years of this century. This terrace, together with Lower Dorington Terrace, was a late nineteenth-century speculative development of artisans' houses.

AN EDWARDIAN SCENE IN HORNS ROAD, Stroud, taken by the Bisley photographer Major. The buildings were another speculative development of artisans' houses.

AN EDWARDIAN VIEW ACROSS THE VALLEY FROM BOWBRIDGE towards the Workhouse (now Stone Manor) prominent on the centre skyline. To its right is The Target Inn and to its left the cemetery chapel. Horns Farm is in the centre.

A VIEW OF BUTTER ROW ALONG BAGPATH ROAD some 50–60 years ago. This lane is one of the old wagon roads on the south side of the valley which provided access to the villages before the present A419 was cut through the valley in 1815.

BUTTER ROW PIKE HOUSE as a village shop some 50–60 years ago. The members of the group are not known, but the boy on the left appears to be wearing a Marling School cap and the girl fifth from the left – a High School hat and blazer. The car has a Bristol registration of the early 1930s.

A BOWBRIDGE VIEW from above the Halt c. 1900–5 towards Park Road and Bowbridge Lane. Middle left, a part of Eagle Mill with, behind it, Ashcroft House, demolished a few years ago and now the site of the recently opened Ashcroft Flats. Upper extreme right is Bowbridge House.

THE RE-MAKING OF BATH ROAD in 1933 between the Rodborough Hill junction and the Clothiers Inn. The base of the chimney of Strachan's Mill in the centre. Behind the support wall on the right stood an old warehouse building which, at this time, would have been Tapper's Repository.

BATH ROAD BEFORE THE FIRST WORLD WAR looking down from the area of the Fromehall Park Road junction. Almost a hive of delivery activity.

A PRE-FIRST WORLD WAR SCENE captured in a picturesque part of Rodborough at the Prince Albert entrance to the Boulevards.

THE SOUTH END OF LIGHTPILL as it was c. 1910–12. Crossing the lower foreground is the Midland Railway to Nailsworth, with the Stroud–Nailsworth road beyond. The group of buildings on the left between the two is the present site of C & J Motors. The three-storey building with the little cottage to its left (left centre) stood at the junction of Kitesnest Lane, the cottage being the old Pike House, demolished for road improvements when the present estates, now covering the fields, were built from the 1950s onwards.

A CLOSE-UP OF THE ROAD IN THE PRECEDING VIEW at approximately the same time – the three-storey building being the one just over the brow.

Rodborough Fort (4)
Stroud

This building was erected by Captain
Hawker in 188_, on a land granted by
the Lord of the Manor. It stands on a bold
eminence, a spur of the Cotswolds, from
which delightful views are to be obtained.
These cover the Stroud Valley, Woodchester,
the Severn Dean Forest, and on clear days
the Sugar Loaf Mountain near Abergavenny.
It is in itself a conspicuous object from
almost every point of the surrounding
neighbourhood

A NOT-SO-COMMON VIEW OF RODBOROUGH FORT issued by Tomkins and Barrett of Swindon.

AN EDWARDIAN SCENE AT RUBBLE HOLE, Little London/Kingscourt. The man in the garden is believed to be Mr Ben Harrison.

Around Stroud

Although perhaps not especially vast in area, such is the village/town density within the Stroud area that to achieve a balanced selection of past scenes in each place would require the wisdom of Solomon, which is much more than we claim to possess. So if any reader feels that we have not done justice to his particular patch, please forgive us. Such is the advantage of today's mobility that he should still enjoy the selection which follows.

AMBERLEY. A scene in 1906. The house on the right is the Amberley Bakery, probably then run by the Smiths. The cart is possibly their own delivery vehicle.

AMBERLEY. The north side of Culver Hill in 1910–12. The entrance to the caves, centre right.

BISLEY. The Bear Inn from the Stroud Road in the 1920s. The driver of the Stroud bus was obviously determined to be in the picture. The old Pound House is on the left.

BISLEY. The pitch leading from the High Street to the churchyard lych gate in winter. Wesley House is on the left. The photograph was a time exposure by moonlight taken in the early 1950s.

THE BOX, probably a 1920s view from near the Half Way House. In the centre, the walled area where the road divides is the Pen. The large house on the right was the home of Baker Daniel whose bakery, partly obscured by trees, was on the opposite side of the road.

THE BOX. A view in the opposite direction, taken from near the church, of approximately the same date. The piece of garden, upper centre right, was where the Mission Hut would be built. On the right skyline is the Half Way House; on the left skyline – the Lealands.

BRIMSCOMBE. An Edwardian view of Brimscombe Hill just below the school and church. On the left the small lean-to is the present shop of Mr Dennis French, wood turner etc. of the Guild of Gloucestershire Craftsmen. The church – Holy Trinity – was built in 1839 and has the altar at the west end. The date is incorporated in the weather vane.

BRIMSCOMBE. An Edwardian view across Brimscombe Corner. Centre right is the gabled front of Brimscombe Mill House, once Biggs Place. The Ship Inn is in line with the telegraph pole on the left. The Victoria and Albert Estates now cover the field behind the row of trees.

BURLEIGH. The view down Brimscombe Hill from the common edge early this century. The Bell Inn is on the roadside, centre, where the road curves to the right.

BROWNSHILL. Thought to be a 1920s scene. The single-storey building behind the trees is the post office; the sub-postmaster would then have been Mr Len Marshall. To the left is Jubilee Terrace and a baker's delivery cart in the road.

BROWNSHILL. The view along Brownshill Road towards the Little House, probably early this century.

BROWNSHILL/BUSSAGE. Brownshill Road; the continuation from the Little House towards Frith Wood, possibly in the early 1920s. The entrance to The Avenue is by the three trees; Redcote Bungalow is on the left. The fields on the left have now been developed.

BUSSAGE. The Avenue at around the same date. Some windows at The Grange, where the celebrated glass engraver Professor Dinkel lived, are visible at the end of the road. The fields on the left are now under development.

CHALFORD. A view from Rack Hill over Sevilles Mill to the Valley Viaduct in the mid 1930s. The Mill was one of the oldest in Chalford. The last woollen cloth being produced there in c. 1860, it was then a silk mill for some 30 years before becoming a site for a wood and bone turning business of Webb & Peacey, which continued until the Second World War. It was demolished by 1952. At the left centre, in a cluster of houses, a bungalow annex with lattice windows can be seen. This annex was originally Kemble East signal box. It was sold to Mr Baughan of Coppice Hill for £6 free delivery by rail to Chalford Station in 1929. He erected it as a sitting room for his daughter and son-in-law. It was demolished a few years ago.

CHALFORD HILL. Jacob's Ladder footpath leading from Marle Hill to Commercial Road c. 1930. The building on the right was once a small mill.

CHALFORD HILL. A 1910–15 view of the west part of the village as seen from behind the Duke of York Inn, the rear garden of which is in the foreground. The buildings in the left foreground, partly hidden by trees, were known as the 'Bunch of Nuts'. The long-roofed building, upper centre right, was The Fleece Inn.

CHALFORD. The west end of Rack Hill c. 1930. On the lower left is the roof of Springfield House Hotel. Above that is the Bell Inn, demolished some 30 years ago, and behind that the Old Brethren Chapel, used as a base for the Dr Foster's Theatre Group until recently. The large field above that – Pooles Ground – was owned by the County Council until the 1950s and was to have been the site for a new junior school. Septic tank drainage for the present County Primary School was provided in the upper right corner of the field before main drainage came to Chalford in the 1960s.

EASTCOMBE. An Edwardian scene in The Street, taken by the Bisley photographer, Major.

EASTCOMBE. Manor Farmhouse, 1919, at the time of the dispersal sale of the Lippiatt Park Estate. The surrounding land once belonging to this farm, has been/is being developed with the Manor School, the Primary School and the Manor and Glevum Estates.

ELCOMBE. A peaceful rural scene, believed to have been taken in the 1920s. The road having ascended from the Vatch, Slad, continues on up the hill past Rose Cottage towards Catswood and Bisley. This was an old road from Gloucester to Cirencester via Painswick, Bisley and Park Corner, Sapperton.

FRANCE LYNCH. A view from the allotments track towards Avenis c. 1937/8. Upper centre is the Court House Inn. The building on the extreme left was then, and still is, the post office. Early this century Mr Young carried on a bakery business here as well as running the shop and post office. The space in front of the building was, for a short while, the terminus of the Red Bus service from Stroud to France Lynch.

THE OPPOSITE VIEW FROM THE PREVIOUS PHOTO at the same time. The cottage lower left was under renovation for Mr Stockley of Bristol. The well-kept garden in the centre was the pride of Mr Baker, a GWR signalman at Frampton Mansell crossing box.

KINGS STANLEY. The area of the green where the village pump stood – just visible on the extreme right – c. 1900–1905.

KINGS STANLEY. The Avenue, St George's, c. 1903.

KINGS STANLEY/LEONARD STANLEY. Bath Road
c. 1906.

LEONARD STANLEY. The area near the church with Church Farm on the right c. 1905.

MINCHINHAMPTON. King Street probably c. 1900. The street is a widened extension of the sunken footpath leading from West End, via the grounds of the Lammas, to Well Hill, the house end on in the centre being the Coffin House. The building, lower right, was demolished fairly early this century.

MINCHINHAMPTON. The Old Forge in Tetbury Street in the early 1920s, in a ruinous condition. The old nameboard of Jehu Shipway is still visible on the wall. Notice the 'owl' window in the gable of the next cottage showing its association with the wool trade.

NAILSWORTH. The junction of Hayes Lane with Northfield Road in 1922/3. Corner Cottage is at the junction.

NAILSWORTH. A view of Forest Green – Northfield area – from Watledge early this century. Upper centre is the Congregational Chapel at the top of Spring Hill, built in 1821 and demolished in 1972.

NAILSWORTH – INCHBROOK. Jeffery's Garage opposite Dunkirk Mills in the late 1930s, a familiar sight on this part of the A46 for many years until demolished in 1963. It was an extension of the original cycle business in Fountain Street. This Inchbrook site is now the forecourt of the Inchbrook Motor Co. The next-door building with the large bay window was once a pub.

THE 'W' NAILSWORTH HILL.

NAILSWORTH. The 'W' probably before 1920. The upper part of the famous Ladder on the left, with Beaudesert Park in the trees.

OAKRIDGE – LILLYHORN. The path from Oakridge through Roborough fields early this century. The white house is Lillyhorn, extensively renovated in the 1930s, and to its left is Lillyhorn Farm.

OAKRIDGE. View from the Bisley Road towards the top of Farm Lane early this century. The triangular green (centre) is where the Dearmer Memorial was to be erected after the First World War.

OAKRIDGE. A view from near the Butcher's Arms over the old mill site to the Whiteway and Whiteway Cottage (centre) probably c. 1920.

FAR OAKRIDGE. The village green complete with maypole in the early years of this century. Everyone in the photograph appears to be posing for the photographer, even the child sitting on the pony's back.

PAINSWICK. St Mary's Street, probably pre-First World War. This small square behind the church illustrates clearly why the town is called the Queen of the Cotswolds.

PAINSWICK. The view down Bisley Street from the A46 crossroads c. 1902–1904. Relatively unchanged to this day in spite of being bombed in the last war.

PAINSWICK. New Street early this century with The Falcon Hotel on the left and the Jubilee lamp in its old island position on the right.

PITCHCOMBE. Resthaven Home of Healing, founded by Miss Maud Carruthers-Little and opened in 1938. This photograph was probably taken soon after the home was opened. Besides being residential, it is also 'open for old & young of all denominations who seek healing in body, mind and spirit.'

RODBOROUGH COMMON. The view from the Bear Hill junction with the Minchinhampton Road, over the Bear Pools to the old house which was demolished to make room for the Bear Pools cafe which, in turn, is still part of the garage complex. Estimated date c. 1920.

RANDWICK. An Edwardian view along The Lane from the rear of the school.

RANDWICK. A late Edwardian view of the school from the churchyard, complete with psuedo Teddy Boy. The bank on the left is the cheese-rolling bank of Wap festivities, though reduced in size now by extensions to the school buildings and grounds.

RUSCOMBE. The Chapel and roads to Whiteshill; estimated to be early this century before, it seems, the single-storey extension building to the Chapel was built.

SLAD. A view from the main road over Vicks Orchard to the road to Steanbridge Mill, c. 1920. The house on the left was Vicks House where, in a lean-to at the far end, there was a small general stores. Fruit from the orchard was sold there in season. The orchard has now been built over.

SELSLEY. The road to Kings Stanley early this century. The photograph appears to have been taken about a quarter of a mile beyond the Church, the thatched cottage having disappeared to be replaced by modern bungalows.

SELSLEY. The west end almost at the parish boundary with Kings Stanley, early this century.

SHEEPSCOMBE. The Flock Mill c. 1900.

STONEHOUSE. The view from the quarry top over the brickworks and the station to the town, probably before 1920.

STONEHOUSE. View SE along the High Street probably in the early 1920s, from approximately where the pedestrian crossing is today. One of those pictures published by G. Timbrell whose shop sign can be seen centre left.

STONEHOUSE. The Midland (Bristol Road) Station yard, date unknown. The stationmaster's house, booking office etc. are on the right. The paved path in the foreground connected the mainline station with the branch line platform to Stroud and Nailsworth.

THRUPP. A view towards Brimscombe along the main road early this century. On the left is the Phoenix Inn, closed many years ago, where now antique and pine furniture etc. is sold. On the right partly hidden by trees, is the Iron Church, erected 1887 as a Chapel-of-Ease to Holy Trinity, Stroud. Now used for the Senior Citizens' Willow Club.

TOADSMOOR. Winter sports on the frozen lake in 1907/8. The Keepers Cottage is across the lake. This lake, nestling in the valley below the Haunted House and fed by the stream rising at the Bisley Wells, is the ancient fish pond of Over Lypiatt manor.

WOODCHESTER – SOUTH. Two opposing views of the same area – the junction of the village road with Atcombe Lane. Above, the shop by the horse and cart is the present Cornerways. The tall two-storeyed house opposite – The Anchorage and Cross House – is that which appears on the right of the picture below. The old house in the centre of the picture below is now almost hidden by trees. Estimated dates are: above – 1920s and below – 1900.

Westrip.

WESTRIP. A view from near Sandpits Lane towards the Carpenters Arms Inn – far right. Probably before 1920.

SECTION FOUR

Schools

Schools were a focal point of community life from Victorian times when churches and chapels vied with one another to provide a smattering of 'free' education to local children, all too often under the guise of religious apartheid.

Only in a part of this selection have we shown the actual school buildings and then only because of their well-known local historical background. Instead we have concentrated on the pupils themselves, selecting, wherever possible, groups whose participants should still be alive today, so that they can enjoy recognising themselves and their contemporaries. Having taken the liberty of naming some of those in the groups, where known to us, we hope we shall not cause offence.

STROUD LIBRARY MEETING ROOM, Lansdown – 1890s. Originally built in 1873 to house the Stroud Grammar School started in 1871 by the Revd A.J. Edmond, curate of Stroud Parish Church. This school closed in 1878 but shortly afterwards was re-opened as the Borough School by Mr Thomas. These schools can be considered to be the main forerunners of Marling School. In 1888 the building was bought by the local clothier – J. Strachan – who gave it to the town as a free library. Currently it caters for a playgroup, is a lecture room for several societies and a meeting place for Stroud Spiritualist Church.

LANSDOWN HALL – 1908. Built in 1879 as a Temperance Hall, as well as being frequently used for public meetings. In 1888 the Borough School transferred here from the adjoining building (above), closing in 1891 when Marling School was opened. By 1892 the Misses Howard had established Stroud High School for Girls here. By 1902 these ladies had a school at Beeches Green called Stroud Ladies College. The building later became the Stroud Christ Scientist Church.

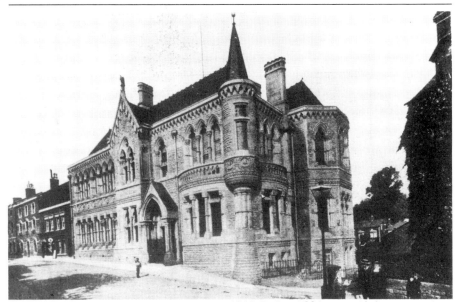

STROUD SCHOOL OF SCIENCE & ART, Lansdown – 1905. Built in 1891 to provide larger premises for the school founded in 1860 in the High Street and providing also a Museum of Natural History. Used in addition by various schools, as in 1904, when Stroud Girls Endowed School was opened here under the headship of Miss D. Beale (niece of the celebrated headmistress of Cheltenham Ladies College), who was later to be the first headmistress of the Stroud Girls High School at Downfield.

THE DOWNFIELD SCHOOLS. An aerial view, c. 1924. Note : there are no buildings for the Girls Central (later Technical) School in the field to the upper right. At that time this school was held in Badbrook Hall and the Stroud School of Art. The move here was to come in 1926/7.

A CLASSROOM OF THE GIRLS ENDOWED SCHOOL in the School of Science & Art in 1906.

MARLING SCHOOL – 1894. There is, as yet, no covered passage between the school and the headmaster's/boarding house. Also the gymnasium has not yet been built.

MARLING SCHOOL PREFECTS – 1926. Left to right standing: R.L.M. Allen, M.R. Mills, L.G. Reynolds, W.W. Barrett. Seated: K.M. Artus, L.A. Ballinger, F.G.N. Smith, J.D.G. Apperley, J.D. Ayres.

MARLING SCHOOL – 1926. The interior of the chemistry laboratory.

STROUD HIGH SCHOOL FOR GIRLS. Official opening of the school by the Duchess of Beaufort, May 1912. Left to right in the doorway: Canon Hawkins, The Duchess, Miss D. Beale the first headmistress and the architect.

STROUD HIGH SCHOOL FOR GIRLS, c. 1912. Unofficially opened in 1911. Compare with p. 75.

STROUD BOYS CENTRAL SCHOOL c. 1930. Originally the Stroud District Craft School opened in 1910. Classrooms 1–3 were in the right-hand building, the two-storey building to the left being for science, art, woodwork and metalwork. The ground floor of this building was used for war work in the First World War. Now it is the Junior School of Marling.

STROUD BOYS CENTRAL SCHOOL. A metalwork class in the school. Believed to be shortly after the school opened. The door in the right-hand wall was the entrance to the gas engine room, the engine driving the belting to power the machinery.

BRIMSCOMBE SECONDARY MODERN SCHOOL c. 1958. Originally the headquarters building of the Thames and Severn Canal. When the canal passed into the ownership of the County Council in the late 1890s, this building was adapted as a polytechnic to train boys and girls in craft skills. It was completely renovated in 1910/11 and continued as Brimscombe Polytechnic until after the Second World War, when it became the Secondary Modern School. The school was transferred to the new Manor School at Eastcombe in 1961.

BRIMSCOMBE POLYTECHNIC. A woodworking class before the First World War.

STRATFORD ABBEY COLLEGE, STROUD, in 1902. The Rose Walk of this girls school is on the right. The principals were the Misses Isacke; Miss Stella celebrated her centenary in 1977. The school was established by Miss Stella's aunts (also the Misses Isacke) in 1869 at Roxburgh House (p. 84) but moved here in 1870. Miss Stella and her two sisters continued to run the school on the retirement of their aunts. The girls wore a distinctive blue uniform. The school closed c. 1940 and the buildings were demolished by c. 1950, the car park of the now-disused Townsends Corn & Seed Mill occupying the site.

STRATFORD ABBEY COLLEGE in 1902. Some of the pupils on the lawn.

ABBOTSFORD COLLEGE, NELSON STREET, STROUD in 1902. A boarding and day school for girls, the principal being Miss Cranstoun. This is now Roxburgh House, the Stroud Youth Centre.

CASTLE STREET SCHOOL, STROUD in 1902. Also known as the Black Boy School due to the statue of the Black Boy in the niche in the gable and above the clock. The clock, which was made by John Miles of Stroud in 1774, was restored by Michael Maltin of Woodchester in 1974. At that time the Black Boy was in a ruinous state. It was a wooden effigy of a negro boy holding a gong in one hand and a club in the other, with which the gong was struck to note the hour. This figure was restored by Patrick Connolly of Cheltenham. On 29 September 1977 it was reported that the clock was striking again. It is thought the effigy was originally some sort of advertisement, e.g. for tobacco, and was adapted to fit the clock. The school is now the Teachers' Centre.

CASTLE STREET SCHOOL. c. 1902. A class of pupils in the yard at the rear. The teacher is thought to be Miss Peer (of the building firm Orchard & Peer).

BISLEY BLUE COAT SCHOOLBOYS – possibly c. 1890 – posed by the Crusaders effigy at Bisley Church. This archway was the entrance to the priests door, bricked up when the church was restored in 1861. The Blue Coat Boys were recipients of the John Taylor Foundation Educational Charity.

BISLEY SCHOOL c. 1912. The cricket team. Note: some of the boys are in the Blue Coat uniform. Left to Right standing: Vince Clarke, Gus Gardiner, Archie Hele, Tom Chew, Sonny Clarke, George Banyard, Smiler Davis, Maurice Skinner, Ebenezer Bloodworth (Headmaster). Seated: Phillip Cooke, Charlie Hook, Jim Clarke (Capt) Ernie Hele, John Jordan.

BRIMSCOMBE SCHOOL c. 1902–5. Left to right, back row: Miss Wilkins (Mrs Newth), Gordon Close, Beattie Dickenson, Kathleen Lodge, Reg Baglin, Phylis Poole, Chrissie Nicholls, Gertie Barrett, Miss House (Mrs Wilkins). Third row: Florrie Wise, Mildred Moon, Margy Halford, Ivy Close, Maudie Philpotts, Willie Ashenford, Olive Clements. Second row: Bernie Cook, Bert King, Charlie King, Lizzie King, George Hind, Ernie Neale, Fred Ashenford, Harry Clements. Front row: Arthur Poole, Maggie Clements, Wilson Saunders, –?–, –?–, Jimmy Clements.

BUSSAGE SCHOOL c. 1932/3.

BUSSAGE HOUSE GIRLS SCHOOL c. mid 1930s. This school was started by Miss Beale and Miss Johnston (5 & 6 from the right in the second row), c. 1912. Miss Beale (see p. 79) and Miss Johnston resigned from the staff of the Stroud High School over a difference of religious opinion and started this school, both remaining at the Bussage House after retirement when the school closed just before the Second World War.

CHALFORD HILL SCHOOL *c.* 1907. Empire Day ceremony of saluting the flag when the song *Flag of Britain* would also have been sung.

CHALFORD HILL SCHOOL c. 1912. The senior boys with the Headmaster Mr Frank (Gaffer) Webster about to start work in the school gardens. The tool shed, made out of old doors, desks etc., remained on the same site for 50 years or so.

CHALFORD CHURCH SCHOOL before 1912. Another Empire Day ceremony. The hatless man (in line with the door) facing the pupils is Mr R.W. Essex, Headmaster, The coachman on the left may have brought either Mrs Ballinger from Skaitshill House to the ceremony or Mr & Mrs Hinton-Jones from The Sevillowes.

EBLEY BRITISH SCHOOL, early 1900s. A class of boys with the headmaster and possibly a pupil-teacher. The school was founded in 1840 by the adjoining Congregational Church. After Ebley Chapel was demolished, church services were, and still are, held here. The school closed when the new Foxmoor School was opened in 1977.

FRANCE LYNCH CHURCH SCHOOL, c. 1925. Left to right, front row: Joan Butler, Rose Cambridge, Freda Minchin, Vera Sherwood, Rose Ford. Middle row: Mr Marmont (Headmaster), Duncan Young, Keith Jackson, Harry Bennett, Ron Minchin, Bill Cambridge, Stanley Steadman. Back row: –?–, Victor Flight, –?–, Harry Peacey.

NAILSWORTH SECONDARY MODERN SCHOOL c. 1953. Interior of a classroom. This was several years before Highwood School was built, when the school used the old junior school in Spring Hill and other buildings.

OAKRIDGE SCHOOL, GROUP 4 in 1935. Left to right, front row: Joan Hunt, Avril Gardiner, Kathleen Powell, Kathleen Stayte, Marjorie Winstone, Freda Bowns, Dorothy Weare, Peggy Weston. Middle row: Reg Venn, Alan Screen, Daisy Phipps, Joan Winstone, Ruby Blackwell, Joyce Long, Dorothy Stayte, Roy Stevens, Peter Hawkins. Back row: Jim Arnold, Alfred Thomas, Roy Young, Gerald Gardiner, Philip Gardiner, Geoffrey Pegler, David Hunt.

RODBOROUGH SCHOOL 1914. The master is thought to be Mr Brown.

SHEEPSCOMBE SCHOOL. Pupils at play early this century.

SECTION FIVE

Churches and Chapels

Many of our old churches were 'modernised', some say 'vandalised', in Victorian times. Fortunately sketches of many of these old churches were made before this process began in 1840 and were later printed as postcards. Other churches replaced chapels of ease or temporary buildings or were built to serve an increasing population.

Likewise many of the non-conformist chapels of today were Victorian enlargements or replacements of earlier buildings which had become too small or delapidated for their congregations.

So in the following selection we have tried to show how some of these old churches/chapels looked, with, where possible, those which replaced them, as well as those which survived with little alteration to the present day.

BISLEY – ALL SAINTS. A sketch, probably by A. Smith c. 1835–40, of the church before restoration, under Thomas Keble the elder, in 1861. Therefore, the church in which the Revd John Keble, the noted Tractarian, was married. Points to note: the outside steps to the galleries in the south aisle, the arched canopy over the priest's door in the south chancel wall and the well-head cover at the left of the picture.

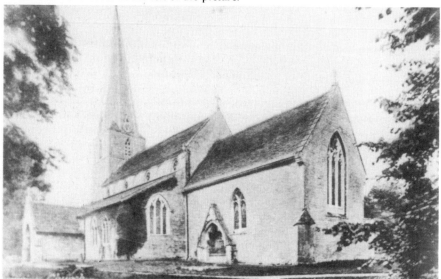

BISLEY – ALL SAINTS. in the early years of this century. Comparison with the previous picture will show the main alterations of the restoration, for example, removal of the galleries, complete rebuilding of the south aisle, alteration of the nave roof-line and the walling in of the priest's door making a niche in which the recumbent effigy of the 'crusader' was placed after removal from the south aisle.

BRIMSCOMBE MISSION CHAPEL, early 1930s. A prominent building at Brimscombe Corner, closed six – eight years ago. It was erected in the 1870s by Mrs Evans, wife of the owner of the Brimscombe Mills complex and the adjacent Silk Mill (now Gordon Terrace). It seems that a debt of several hundred pounds was owed to the business when the books were closed for audit, which was thought to be non-recoverable. However within a year or so the debt was paid in full and Mrs Evans was given the money to use for any project she desired. The building of this chapel was the project. The figure standing in this photograph is Pastor Gregory Hopper, who was also pastor at Box Mission Hall.

BROWNSHILL. The two corrugated iron buildings which have been known as the two 'tin chapels'. The one on the right has been an evangelical mission hall all this century, closing only some two years ago. The one on the left has had some associations with it in the distant past, but has been a private dwelling for very many years. It is thought to be the iron chapel erected in 1900 as a small chapel of ease to Christ Church, Chalford, through the efforts of Mr Sawyer who was given the oversight.

BUSSAGE – ST MICHAEL AND ALL ANGELS. south aspect, c. 1950. Built in 1844/6, being the second of the churches built by Thomas Keble, vicar of Bisley, to serve remote areas of his vast parish. Its foundation was due to the efforts of 20 Oxford scholars, who set aside a portion of their income for 5 years. This is recorded in Latin on the foundation stone, a translation of the final part being: 'built at the sole expense of twenty scholars of the University of Oxford. Unknown in this place, but known to God'. The south aisle, designed by Bodley, was added in 1854 and the clock commemorated Queen Victoria's Diamond Jubilee.

CHALFORD TABERNACLE. the Baptist Chapel, c. 1907, the person in the picture being Mr Simmonds of Chalford Hill. The chapel, in a prominent position in Coppice Hill, was built in 1873/4, chiefly through the beneficence of William and Eleanor Dangerfield of Bliss Mills. It replaced the eighteenth-century Copse Chapel just below, still used as a meeting room/manse flat. This tabernacle is still used for special services.

CHALFORD – CHRIST CHURCH. An early 1900s view. Built 1724 as a chapel of ease it was reconstructed in 1841 and given its own parish. It is relatively unchanged in style today, unlike the scene on the opposite side of the road. The blacksmith's forge etc. on the left of the road were demolished in the 1960s for road widening and much of the canal filled in. The road support wall, built when the original road was made in 1815, is still there, buried under the now widened road.

A HILLY VIEW. CHALFORD.   CLB23

CHALFORD, WESLEYAN CHAPEL. A photograph of the 1930s when the chapel was still in use.
Occupying a prominent position behind the Chalford bus terminus, it was built in 1858/9 to
replace an older building but, through lack of support, it finally closed c. 1957. It has been
used since as a private dwelling/studio by a succession of owners.

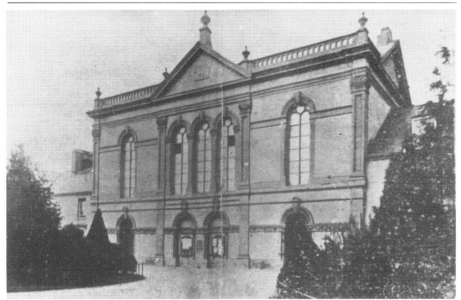

EBLEY CONGREGATIONAL CHAPEL. An early 1900s view. Built in 1881 to replace the earlier one built in 1797. A fine building, demolished around 1970 becaue of structural decay. The congregation now meets in the adjoining buildings, once the Ebley School (see p. 92).

FRANCE LYNCH – ST JOHN THE BAPTIST. A view of c. 1905. It was the last of the churches built by Keble for his vast parish, the instigator being one of his curates – Edward Pyddoke. Built in 1857, Pyddoke became the first priest in charge as it remained a chapel of ease until 1897. It was the first local church to be designed by the architect Bodley.

FRANCE LYNCH – THE OLD VESTRY. An artist's impression, by A.E. Phelps, of the last building which stood on this site – the oldest Dissenters' chapel in the ancient Bisley parish. The first building was erected in 1697 and replaced by the second during the eighteenth century. By 1819 this building was too small and stone from it was used to build a new chapel a few hundred yards away (see below). The sunday school, which had been adjacent to the second building, was rebuilt over part of the site of this eighteenth-century chapel and was used for mid-week meetings and also as a day-school. This sketch shows that building which was demolished in the 1870s.

CHALFORD HILL – FRANCE CONGREGATIONAL CHAPEL. Built in 1819 (see above), the adjoining sunday school rooms on the right being added in the 1850s. The appearance of the burial ground suggests this photograph was taken at about the time of the Second World War. Through lack of support the church was closed in October 1985 and the buildings have now been sold for conversion into private dwellings.

AN OLD COTSWOLD HOME.

MINCHINHAMPTON – HOLY TRINITY. Probably another of the sketches by A. Smith. A church has been here since Norman times, the medieval church being 'ruthlessly' restored in 1842. The tower presents a problem to the historian – did it have a spire? Atkyns and Rudder say 'Yes', but it was taken down and rebuilt to this form. Others say it was always this short form. An interesting part of the sketch is the building to the right – the old Mansion. According to Playne it was originally a farm which was enlarged by the clothier Philip Shepherd to become his family seat.

LEONARD STANLEY – ST SWITHINS. Another sketch by A. Smith, probably 1835–40. One of the oldest churches in the district, it remains relatively unspoilt by Victorian fervour. It was built very close to an old Saxon church, remains of which are incorporated into the adjoining Priory Farm buildings.

LEONARD STANLEY – METHODIST CHAPEL. Not a close-up, but in this picture, taken from the church tower probably early this century, the chapel can be seen upper left centre.

NAILSWORTH – SHORTWOOD CHAPEL. A sketch of the first Baptist mission house built in 1716 and subsequently enlarged. It was demolished in 1837 to make room for the larger second Baptist chapel. That in turn was demolished in 1887 when the third chapel – now Christ Church – was built in Newmarket Road. The original meeting was an offshoot of the Baptist meeting at Kings Stanley. In turn, Shortwood meeting was the mother meeting of the Minchinhampton Baptist meeting.

NAILSWORTH – ST GEORGE. A sketch, probably of the late 1890s, of the proposed church which was to replace the old Pepperpot Church on the same site. It seems that the ground was found to be too unstable to support the weight of the tower so the latter was redesigned to make the large porch entrance we know today.

OAKRIDGE – ST BARTHOLOMEW. Probably another of A. Smith's sketches of the 1835–40 period. This church was the first of the churches built by Thomas Keble to serve his vast parish. It was opened in 1835 as a chapel of ease, acquiring its own parish in 1842. It celebrated its 150th anniversary on 24 August 1987.

SHEEPSCOMBE – ST JOHN. A view of 1902. The church was built in 1820 and enlarged in 1872.

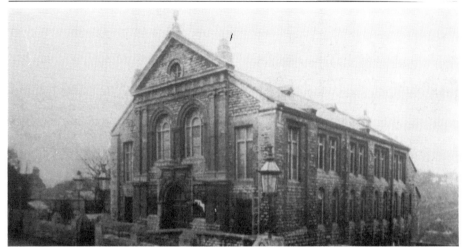

STROUD – CASTLE STREET METHODIST CHAPEL. Built in 1875/6 by George Drew, Builders, of Chalford. The foundation stone was laid by Mr (later Sir) S.S. Marling in September, 1875. The Wesleyans had formerly worshipped in the round building – opened in 1763 – in Acre Street and which is now The Citadel of the Salvation Army. The chapel was closed some years ago but planning permission for conversion to 18 flats has recently been given.

STROUD – OLD CHAPEL CONGREGATIONAL. The interior c. 1903. This chapel stood in Chapel Street, near the present Parliament Street School, and was the oldest Dissenting place of worship in the town. It was built c. 1710 to replace an earlier meeting house. The latter had been converted from an old barn and stood close to where the Top of the Town Car Park is today. Bedford Street Chapel is a daughter chapel built in 1837 because of overcrowding at Old Chapel. The Old Chapel was closed about 1970 and demolished when the Chapel Street area was redeveloped. The present day Pentecostal church occupies the Old Chapel Sunday School buildings built c. 1820.

STROUD – ST LAWRENCE. Probably another of A. Smith's sketches showing how Stroud's parish church looked before the restoration of 1866–68. Originally built in the fourteenth century as a chapel of ease to All Saints, Bisley, it was continually added to over the years. The tall west spire contained ten bells. The small spire to the east was at the end of the original chancel and contained two bells. The whole building, except the west spire, was demolished and rebuilt in the restoration.

STROUD – UPLANDS – ALL SAINTS. Built 1908–10, the architect being Temple Moore and the builders, Messrs Gardner & Sons of Stroud. The tower and spire were added later in the early 1920s, which dates this photograph to the second decade of this century.

STROUD – UPLANDS – ALL SAINTS IRON CHURCH. A view from Folly Lane, probably c. 1900–5. This would have been the second iron building, erected by T.M. Croome to replace the smaller one, originally owned by the Revd Thomas Wintle, which had stood near Hawthorn Cottage in Slad Road. This church served as a chapel of ease to Slad Church and had a resident curate. In 1875 Croome sold the building to a committee, headed by W. Capel of The Grove, which had been set up to promote the building of a new stone church for Uplands. The latter was eventually built (see p. 108), and this iron building was sold, presumably to Stonehouse Church, for it was erected in Laburnum Walk, Stonehouse, as a church hall. In approximately 1934, it was opened as the Regal Cinema, but was burnt out in a disastrous fire on 18 September 1936.

STONEHOUSE – CONGREGATIONAL CHAPEL. This chapel was built in the High Street in 1827, the date of this photograph being 1945. It closed in 1964 and was burnt down in 1967. Its site is now occupied by the Nat West Bank and adjoining buildings.

WOODCHESTER – ST MARY. The old Norman church which stood on the Roman villa site. By 1859 it was in a very ruinous state and the decision was made to demolish it and use the stone to build a new church about a quarter of a mile away. Demolition commenced in 1861, the new church being consecrated in 1863.

WOODCHESTER – ST MARY. An interior view of the old church showing the low chancel arch, remains of which still stand in the old churchyard where the Roman pavement lies buried. Gloucestershire Church Notes of 1851 say 'the church is frightfully encumbered with hideous pews and galleries'. The memorial tablets were transferred to the new church when the old church was demolished.

Public Houses

Yet one more focal point of community life that is very different today. Probably many of the pubs originated as ale-houses selling beer (or cider) brewed on the premises. Later they would have become tied to small breweries such as Watts and Godsells, of Stroud, Carpenters of Cainscross, Clissolds of Nailsworth, Smiths of Brimscombe and Playnes of Minchinhampton. In turn, all these disappeared through amalgamation, eventually becoming a part of the giants such as Whitbread/ Flowers. Then, almost inevitably, many closures of pubs followed on economic grounds, although some survived in private hands as 'free houses' and some were revamped to produce today's chrome-plated image.

Here we have selected views of many which are no longer pubs, together with a few well-known ones which have survived – generally with a much altered façade.

THE BEAR HOTEL, RODBOROUGH. A not so well known view of the Hotel as it was c. 1905.

BISLEY, The Bell in the High Street with landlord Sherwood standing under the sign – early 1900s. The Bell has been closed for very many years and is now the headquarters of the Bisley branch of the British Legion. Part of the building is also being used as a branch surgery for the Eastcombe group of doctors.

BISLEY, The George in the High Street opposite George Street, in the early 1900s when it was a Nailsworth Brewery House. In the bowler hat is landlord Harry Cook; in the top hat is Bogey Jones the jobbing gardener. Closed a few years ago, it is now the post office and village stores.

THE BOX – The Halfway House – as it was probably just before the First World War.

THE BOX – probably a 1920s photograph. Just left of centre, with the brewery sign partly hidden, is the Box Inn, closed in 1967. The fields and rickyard in the foreground belonged to Joe Norton, son of the tenant of the Halfway House.

THE BOX – probably a 1920s photograph taken from the bank near the Halfway House towards Box Farm (centre skyline). The three-gabled house (upper left centre) was, in the nineteenth century, the Beehive Inn. It was later the home of Mr Mortimer, who was both a butcher, with shop and slaughter house adjacent, and also a dairy farmer, supplying milk to Box residents. The inn sign carried a doggerel which was, apparently, not unique to this inn. It ran:

> In this Beehive we're all alive
> Good liquor makes you funny
> If you are dry, step in and try
> The flavour of our honey.

BRIMSCOMBE – THE YEW TREE, Wallsquarry – probably c. 1912–15. It was closed a few years ago and is now a private house, although planning permission to open a small cafe here is currently being sought. The group of white buildings above the horse van is The Bell at Burleigh – also closed.

BROWNSHILL – THE RAILWAY TAVERN – St Mary's Way as it was early this century. Although sited several hundred feet above Brimscombe Station, it was so called as it stood opposite the footpath which descended through Brownshill Banks to the main road by the Victoria Inn (now The King and Castle Hotel). Brimscombe Station served Brownshill.

CAINSCROSS. The Spring at the bottom of Paganhill Lane – probably 1920s. Although a Stroud house here, it could have run a pipeline to Cainscross Brewery which was behind it.

CHALFORD – THE COMPANYS ARMS – c. 1935. One of the oldest houses in Chalford, it has now reverted to a private house under its old name of Chalford Place. It became an inn in the late eighteenth century, finally closing in 1964. The name illustrated the connection of so much of the cloth trade around Stroud with the East India Company. In the early nineteenth century it was a coaching inn, running coaches to London and Gloucester and thrice weekly to Bristol, their fine qualities being described by the boys of the day as:

A bandy-legged coachman
A wooden-legged guard
And three blind horses,
That could not run a yard.

CHALFORD – THE VALLEY – lower right – c. 1907 when it was a house of Brimscombe Brewery. Formerly called the Clothiers Arms it was originally a clothier's house. It was closed in 1969 and is now a private house.

CHALFORD HILL – THE FLEECE INN – as a Brimscombe Brewery house early this century. Closed in 1939 it is now a private house. The donkeys standing at the end of Commercial Road were used for coal delivery by J.H. Smart & Sons of Chalford Wharf. His children are standing by the donkeys.

CHALFORD HILL – MECHANICS ARMS – in Midway, as it was in the second decade of this century. The landlord Mr Whiting and his housekeeper, Miss Nash. The storehouse to the left is now part of the modernised inn.

EASTCOMBE – THE RED LION – probably a photograph of the second decade. The landlord was Arthur Davis. It was closed, we believe, around the end of the First World War.

EBLEY – THE COACH & HORSES. Still going strong on the A419 opposite Cordwells Garage, but this is how it appeared in the mid 1920s.

FAR OAKRIDGE – THE NELSON as it was in the 1940s. It stood at the junction of the Daneway and Iles Green Roads and closed in 1959.

FRANCE LYNCH – THE COURT HOUSE in the 1930s when Mrs Butler was the landlady. The origin of the name is obscure but it may have been the venue for manorial courts of the Bisley sub-manor of Sturmyes Court. It had been an Inn certainly from the 1880s. It closed in 1956, the last landlord being Mr Ron Clissold.

HYDE – THE RAGGED COT as it was in the early 1920s probably when Mr Cox was landlord. It has been greatly enlarged and modernised in recent years.

MINCHINHAMPTON – THE SALUTATION, TETBURY STREET. Closed by 1965 when the firm of F.A. Wall & Sons moved their electrical TV business there from the top of Tetbury Street. This photograph pictures the Inn as it was in the 1920s.

PITCHCOMBE – THE EAGLE, C. 1927. This Inn was some distance from the centre of the village, standing on the A46, which curves on the left towards Painswick. Left to right: Harry Jones, a Customer, Landlord John Jones, Rona Jones, Josie Jones. It was closed some years ago.

LEONARD STANLEY – THE LAMB. An early 1900s photograph taken from the Stonehouse Road. It was closed in 1982.

STROUD, THE POST OFFICE – opposite the Subscription Rooms in George Street as it was in the mid 1920s. Before it become an Inn the building was Stroud's first Post Office, standing from the 1840s to the 1880s when it became too small. The second Post Office was then built in Russell Street, c. 1885.

WOODCHESTER – THE TEN BELLS, at Frogmarsh in 1905. The sign can be seen below the gables and over the top of the hay-rick. It was closed in 1924.

WATERLANE – THE CROWN as it was in the 1950s. The upper road in the photograph leads to Tunley and Daneway. The pub was closed in 1969 and the last landlady was Mrs Howkins.

Individuals and Groups

All communities had well-known individuals some of whom, perhaps, were well-known because of their eccentricity, others just because they epitomised a hardworking but perhaps serene life-style. We hope that the pictures which follow illustrate these points, as well as bringing back memories to older readers.What better way to start than with two of the area's photographers who left us such a legacy.

Groups are perhaps more difficult to select so we have tried to show different facets of Stroud life and could not resist including Football Teams, though we have been somewhat biased towards our area in our collection.

FRANK COLVILLE AND HIS WIFE. A Chalford photographer in the early years of this century, moving to Swindon in the 1920s, as will be seen from this photograph.

WELL-KNOWN INHABITANTS OF ASHMEADS, Chalford – George & Dorcas Juggins, photographed in the 1960s, at their evening 'spiritual' home – the Butchers Arms at Oakridge. Dorcas was the only child of Townsends who ran horse buses from Chalford to Stroud and Cirencester early this century. George was a Brimscombe lad. Dorcas met a sad end by being burnt to death in February 1975 when her home was gutted during the night. George had died several years before.

THE STROUD PHOTOGRAPHER, H.J. COMLEY of Russell Street.

ALFRED BUCKNELL – blacksmith and metal craftsman of Waterlane – as a young man in the 1890s. Probably not many years before he joined the Ernest Gimson team at Daneway House to make ironwork to Gimson's designs.

BOB GASTON, the Eastcombe/Bisley postman, taken on his rounds in the early years of this century. He retired from the Postal Service in 1922.

NO RECORD OF GEORGE AND DORCAS JUGGINS WOULD BE COMPLETE (see p. 128) without a photograph of his mother-in-law, whom George had to push from Chalford to Stroud in her wheel chair, every week. Here they are, we believe near the Capital and Counties Bank probably in the 1920s. It was from outside the Greyhound Inn that, after an altercation with mother-in-law, George is alleged to have given the chair a push to send both careering down Gloucester Street.

MR JEFFERIES OF EBLEY, undated but probably early this century.

NURSE MANFELL, Bisley District Nurse. Undated but thought to be early this century.

ALFRED SOLLARS of Eastcombe photographed probably in the 1930s. A lifetime resident of Eastcombe, he worked for Ewart Bingle on the timber wagons.

SGT. G.R.R. RATCLIFFE OF BISLEY, C. 1880 in the dress uniform of the Royal Gloucester Yeomanry. He farmed at Stancombe, Bisley in later years. His daughter Mary married Fred Clarke who kept the village stores and Post Office in Bisley for many years.

FRED GARDINER OF OAKRIDGE, another craftsman/furniture maker of the Gimson school and later member of the Peter van der Waals team.

JOHN HAWKES OF CHALFORD HILL, organist of Bussage Church from 1896 for almost 60 years. One of a musical family, his brother Archie was a stalwart member of Chalford Brass/Silver Band. For many years he was one of Chalford's postmen (see p. 145).

SIR ROBERT (BOBBY) PERKINS — Stroud's MP, from 1931–1945 and 1950–1955. Living at Rookswood on the Holy Brook, Bisley, he flew his own plane from a field adjoining Limekiln Lane between Bisley and Waterlane.

MR EDWIN HUNT AND HIS WIFE OF BOURNES GREEN, Oakridge, photographed probably around 1900. He farmed at Bournes Green.

WILLIAM & MARTHA GARDINER OF OAKRIDGE at hay-making time. William was a brother of Eli, mentioned by Sir William Rothenstein in his autobiography *Men and Memories* as 'knew his Bible, the Old Testament especially and could interpret the sign of the skies, the sun, clouds and the flight of birds – and he knew the secret of life of field and hedgerow'.

JOHN PEACEY OF OAKRIDGE, born 1844, died 1936. He started work when seven years old in Ashmeads Silk Mill and then, as a young man, at Benjamin Gardiner's boat yard at Framilode. He walked from Oakridge to Framilode to begin at 8a.m. on a Monday morning and lodged locally during the week to start work at 4a.m. He left to work at Bliss Mills, Chalford, at the age of 25 considering this to be a more stable foundation for married life. Later he started a bakery and village general stores in Oakridge. He was the stalwart of Oakridge Methodist Church for many years.

GIPSY PEGLER OF PAINSWICK who lived in his caravan at the lower side of the Plantation. A true gypsy; his caravan was burnt on his death. Known to his contempories as a very congenial man and as honest as the day.

MRS BANKS crowning the Bisley Flower Show Queen – Linda Jane Maller – early 1970s. The Revd P. Ettrick, Vicar of Bisley is on the left.

BRIMSCOMBE CHURCH MOTHER'S UNION, late 1930s.

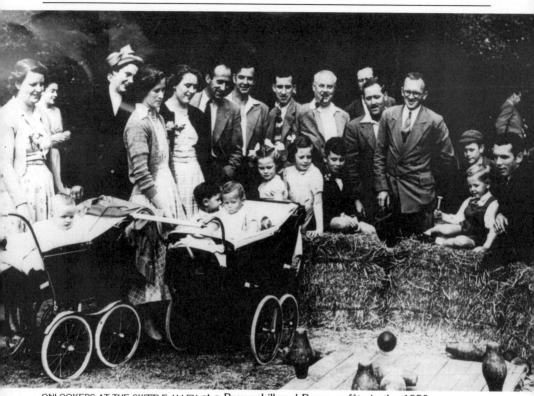

ONLOOKERS AT THE SKITTLE ALLEY at a Brownshill and Bussage fête in the 1950s.

CHALFORD POST OFFICE STAFF, 1935. Left to right, standing: Doug Rowles, Len Freeman, Bill Fern, Fred Fry, George Young. Seated: John Hawkes, Stan Cook (Sub-Postmaster), Reg Blackwell.

EBLEY GIRL GUIDES dressed up for what? The photograph is believed to have been taken in the late 1920s.

OAKRIDGE VILLAGE PLAYERS — cast of the play, *Hunsdon House*, written by Lady Darwin. Produced by Sir (then Mr) William Rothenstein and dated the second decade. Left to right, standing: Walter Wood, May Wear, Harry Davoll, Fred Gardiner, Tom Gardiner, Jim Gardiner, William Allen. Seated: Louisa Gardiner, Walter Young, M. Gardiner, Kate Young.

PAINSWICK CURIOS, 1904. The Bow Wow Banner and the Stocks. The name of the man in the stocks was given as Gypsy Ryalls, but appears to be the Gypsy Pegler of p. 141. The banner is connected with the Old Painswick Feast Sunday when it was a custom of the inhabitants to eat a plum pie in which a small china dog has been placed prior to baking. Arising from this, Hyett quotes three stories about dogs being killed and served up in pies. Stroud youths apparently shouted 'Bow Wow' to Painswick youths when they met, probably leading to a fight.

SLAD WI, C. 1930. Left to right, back row: –?–, Miss Dunham, –?–, Gladys Tilley. Middle row : Mrs Dickenson, ? Davis. Mrs Fern, Mrs Norman Vick, Mrs Green, Mary Dyer. Front row: –?–, Miss Golding (Jnr schoolmistress), Miss Wardley, Mrs Stafford, Mrs Dickenson?

SOME OF THE PLAYERS FROM STONEHOUSE, the Stanleys and Eastington who took part in Episode I of the Mid-Gloucestershire Historical Pageant of Progress at Fromehall Park, Stroud, on 2 September 1911. Episode I was entitled 'Britons and Romans – *circa* AD 45'.

END OF WAR CELEBRATIONS at Rodborough in 1945. Middle Spillmans Gypsies outside the Endowed Schools.

FÊTE DAY at Stonehouse – the dress suggests the 1920s.

EMPLOYEES OF WM. SELWYN'S FLOCK MILL at Toadsmoor, early 1900s.

A FINE BODY OF MEN – the Police of Stroud Division, probably around 1900–05. Inset: Supt. Biggs. Left to right, back row: PCs Sandalls, Dance, William, Merrett, Philips, Hughes, Lacey McKnight and Garner. Middle row: PCs Brotheridge, Jones, Grinnell, Ash. Drill Instr. Hayward, PCs Hayward, Church, Ogborne, Midhurst, Wintle, Neale. Front row: PCs Rhead, Spicer, Gale. P.Sgt. Hale, P.Sgt. Smith, Supt. Biggs P.Sgt. Packer, P.Sgt. Cook PCs Gabb, Reubensen, Townsend. Lying down: PCs Greengrass, Simpson.

BRIMSCOMBE (THE LILYWHITES) SECOND XI, with Club Officials and Referee – 1933/4. Left to right, Club Officials and Referee: J. Hanks, H. Pearce, K. Knight, L. Gardiner, E. David, F. King, W. Ponting, W. Griffin. Team standing: B. Fry, W. Phillips, F. Ponting, H. Wilkins. Seated: C. Bignell, R. Ponting, K. Fletcher, B. Tilley, C. Fletcher. On the grass: J. Warren, L. Randall.

BUSSAGE AFC. 1925/6. Left to right, standing: R. Butler, T. Bird, R. Clissold, C. Riches, H. Riches, W. Clissold, E. Butler. Seated: S. Shepherd, S. Watkins, E. Clissold, Baggy Butler, Front row: F. Neale, H. Munday, G. Wall, E. Davis, J. Matthews.

CAINSCROSS AND EBLEY AFC 1911/12.

CHALFORD AFC in the late 1940s. Left to right, standing: Ron Davis, Percy Abel, Jack Ridiford, Len Kibble, P. Hill, D. Shergold, Ernie Young, Ben Baxter. Kneeling: Fred Townsend, Alan Smith, Wilf Townsend, Frank Gardiner, Les Kirby.

WHAT IS THIS BEVY OF CHALFORD BEAUTIES UP TO, c. 1950? Outside the Mechanics Arms too! Although that was the changing rooms of Chalford AFC when they played at the Sycamores.

RODBOROUGH OLD BOYS AFC, 1919.

STROUD MOTOR CYCLE FOOTBALL TEAM, 1930s, probably at Fromehall Park where their home games were played. Left to right: W. Griffiths, J. Hogg, C. Stagg, T. Powles, E. Turner, J. Lasbury, N. Burrows.

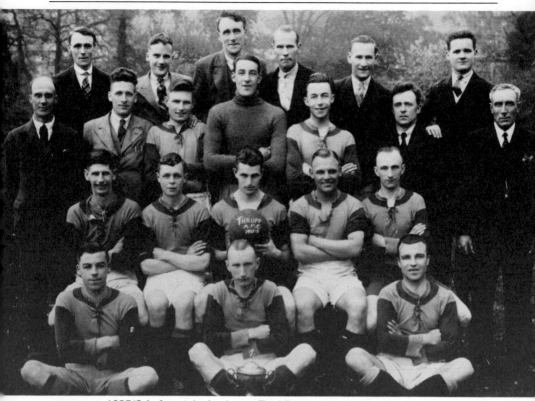

THRUPP AFC, 1935/6. Left to right, back row: Fred Baxter, Harold May, George Neale, Lou Fry, A. Stevens, John Roberts. Third row: Arthur Jackson, Les Gardiner, George Strange, –?–, –?–, Owen Pegler, Mr Fry. Second row: R. King, Arthur Wakeman, Jack Riddiford, Maurice Woods, Stan Savage. Front row : Les Hook, Fred Savage, C. Bignell.

PHOTOGRAPH CREDITS

Dr R. Allen • R. Arnold • G. Askew • H. Beard • Miss Benjamin • R. Bingle
Mrs Bishop • Mrs Blacktin • Mrs J. Blanshard • Revd J. Bourne •
Miss D. Brimfield • Mrs Clark • D. Clarke • R. Clarke • P. Clissold • R. Cook
Mrs S. Cove • R. Cratchley • Mrs Y. Crew • Mrs Dangerfield • Miss J. Davis
W. Davis • J. Denley • Mrs J. Flint • Revd J. Forryan • Mrs Franklin • J. Garner
G. Gleed • M. Goodenough • Mrs Greening • P. Griffiths • E. Harper • J. Histed
K. Hitchings • Miss M. Hook • Mrs Hunt • J. Ireland • O. Jeffery • Mrs G. Jellyman
A. Lasbury • A. Liddiatt • W. Merrett • Mrs E. Mills • M. Mills • Miss Milne
Mrs J. Sampson • K. Shaylor • Mrs A. Sollars • J. Stephens • Mrs Stockbridge
Mrs J. Sturm • Mrs J. Tanner • Mrs Townsend • R. Turner • Miss Wallis
Mrs White • Mrs J. Young • W.D. Young • and the late G. Juggins • A. Mutton
J. Riddiford • G. St John Sanders.

GLOUCESTERSHIRE IN OLD PHOTOGRAPHS

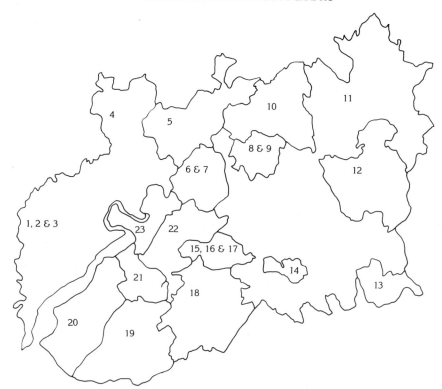